Pebble Plus

The U.S. Senate

by Mari Schuh

Consulting Editor: Gail Saunders-Smith, PhD

Consultant: Steven S. Smith, Kate M. Gregg Distinguished Professor
of Social Sciences and Professor of Political Science
Director, Weidenbaum Center on the Economy, Government, and Public Policy
Washington University, St. Louis, Missouri

CAPSTONE PRESS
a capstone imprint

Pebble Plus is published by Capstone Press,
1710 Roe Crest Drive, North Mankato, Minnesota 56003.
www.capstonepub.com

Books published by Capstone Press are manufactured with paper
containing at least 10 percent post-consumer waste.

Library of Congress Cataloging-in-Publication Data
Schuh, Mari C., 1975–
  The U.S. Senate / by Mari Schuh.
    p. cm.—(Pebble plus. The U.S. government)
  Includes bibliographical references and index.
  Summary: "Simple text and full-color photographs provide a brief introduction to the U.S. Senate"—Provided by
publisher.
  ISBN 978-1-4296-7567-3 (library binding)
  1. United States. Congress. Senate—Juvenile literature. 2. Legislators—United States—Juvenile literature. I. Title. II.
Title: US Senate. III. Title: United States Senate.
  JK1276.S35 2012
  328.73'071—dc23

2011021663

Editorial Credits
Erika L. Shores, editor; Ashlee Suker, designer; Kathy McColley, production specialist

Photo Credits
Getty Images/Chip Somodevilla, 13; El Universal, 7; Joe Raedle, 11; Justin Sullivan, 15; Mark Wilson, 17;
    Roll Call/Tom Williams, 5
newscom/Blackstar/Owen, 21; Getty Images/AFP/Tim Sloan, 19
Official White House photo by Pete Souza, 9
Shutterstock/fstockfoto, cover, 1

Artistic Effects
Shutterstock: Christophe BOISSON

The author dedicates this book to her husband, Joseph Quam.

Note to Parents and Teachers

The U.S. Government series supports national history standards related to understanding the
importance of and basic principles of American democracy. This book describes and illustrates
the U.S. Senate. The images support early readers in understanding the text. The repetition of
words and phrases helps early readers learn new words. This book also introduces early readers
to subject-specific vocabulary words, which are defined in the Glossary section. Early readers
may need assistance to read some words and to use the Table of Contents, Glossary, Read
More, Internet Sites, and Index sections of the book.

Printed in the United States of America in North Mankato, Minnesota.
102011   006405CGS12

Table of Contents

Making Laws 4

Three Branches 6

Becoming a Senator. 10

Senators at Work 14

Glossary 22

Read More 23

Internet Sites. 23

Index 24

Making Laws

The U.S. Senate works in Washington, D.C., to write bills. Bills are plans for new laws. Bills are about schools, health care, safety, and other issues.

Three Branches

The U.S. government has three branches. Congress is the legislative branch. The Senate and the House of Representatives make up Congress.

The executive branch puts laws into effect and makes sure people follow them. The president heads this branch. The judicial branch explains the laws.

Becoming a Senator

Each U.S. state elects two senators. Senators represent the people of their home states. Senators serve a term of six years. They can be elected again and again.

Senators must be at least

30 years old. They need to

be U.S. citizens for at least

nine years. They need to live in

the state where they are elected.

Senators at Work

Senators talk with people
in their home state.
Senators learn what
new laws people want.

Senators work on committees

to study new bills.

Senators meet with

the president, give speeches,

and vote on treaties.

MS. KLOBUCHAR

17

The vice president is
the head of the Senate.
His only role is to vote
on bills when there is a tie.

The Senate and the House need to pass the same bill. If the president signs the bill, it becomes a new law.

Glossary

bill—a written plan for a new law; the U.S. Senate and the House of Representatives write bills

committee—a small group of people chosen to discuss things and make decisions for a larger group

elect—to choose someone by voting

executive branch—the part of the U.S. government that performs duties required by laws and makes sure people follow the laws

House of Representatives—a part of the U.S. government that makes laws, along with the Senate

judicial branch—the part of the U.S. government that explains the laws; the courts make up this branch

law—a rule made by the government that must be obeyed

term—a set period of time elected leaders serve in office

treaty—an official agreement between two or more countries

Read More

Gorman, Jacqueline Laks. *Member of Congress.* Know Your Government. Pleasantville, N.Y.: Weekly Reader, 2009.

Harris, Nancy. *What's Congress?* First Guide to Government. Chicago: Heinemann Library, 2007.

Jakubiak, David J. *What Does a Senator Do?* How Our Government Works. New York: PowerKids Press, 2010.

Internet Sites

FactHound offers a safe, fun way to find Internet sites related to this book. All of the sites on FactHound have been researched by our staff.

Here's all you do:

Visit *www.facthound.com*

Type in this code: 9781429675673

Check out projects, games and lots more at
www.capstonekids.com

Index

bills, 4, 16, 18, 20
committees, 16
Congress, 6
election, 10, 12
executive branch, 8
health care, 4
House of Representatives,
  6, 20
judicial branch, 8
laws, 4, 8, 14, 20

legislative branch, 6
president, 8, 16, 20
safety, 4
schools, 4
speeches, 16
states, 10, 12, 14
terms, 10
ties, 18
treaties, 16
vice president, 18

Word Count: 207
Grade: 1
Early-Intervention Level: 20